...ca of Saint Francis

A Spiritual Pilgrimage

Text:
Xavier Goulet OFM CONV.
Ciaran McInally OFM CONV.
Joseph Wood OFM CONV.

Nihil obstat: imprimatur
Assisi 31 marzo 1994

P. Giulio Berrettoni
Custode della Basilica
di S. Francesco

© CASA EDITRICE FRANCESCANA - ASSISI

Printed in Italy - Tipografia Metastasio - Assisi

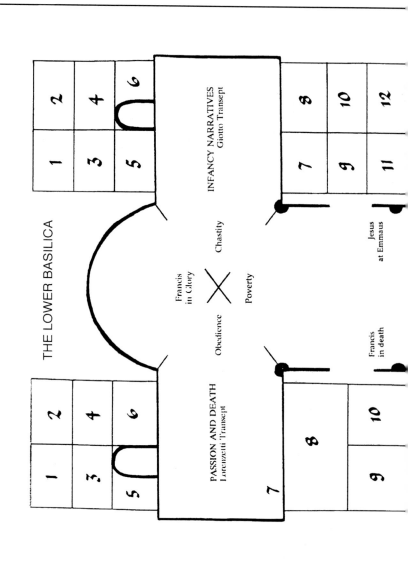

THE LOWER BASILICA

INFANCY NARRATIVES
Giotto Transept

PASSION AND DEATH
Lorenzetti Transept

Francis
in Glory

Obedience

Chastity

Poverty

Jesus
at Emmaus

Francis
in death

1 2
3 4
5 6

1 2
3 4
5 6

7 8
9 10
11 12

7
8
9 10

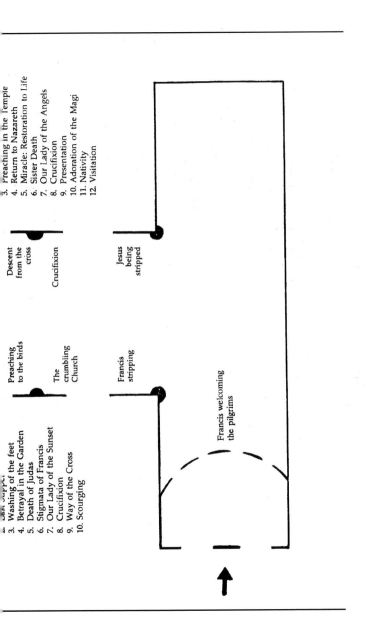

The Basilica of Saint Francis
A Spiritual Pilgrimage

Probably no city in Christendom has been so thoroughly identified with its saint as Assisi has been identified with Saint Francis. Through the centuries Assisi has been described by an impressive array of authors as, "One of the most holy cities of our western world;" "The town at whose feet everything bad dies;" "A citadel of the spirit;" "A city of light;" "A particle of paradise." Johannes Jorgensen, an early biographer, and a long time local resident, said that in Assisi, he "sat at Francis' feet and entered heaven."

For pilgrim and tourist alike, the basilica of Saint Francis offers the best means of entry into the mystery of Assisi and of its *Poverello*, "the little poor man," Francesco. As our body can enter into the town through any one of the picturesque gates in the medieval wall it is only through poetry and art that our soul can penetrate its mystery.

This small publication is intended as a spiritual journey through the basilica of Saint Francis. This booklet is a pilgrim's guide for a journey inward, for it is only inward that one discovers the greatest art, the hidden treasure, which is the abiding presence of the one true God.

A Brief Historical Appreciation

Saint Francis of Assisi died on the evening of 3 October 1226. Two years after his death, 30 March 1228, Brother Elias of Assisi, Francis' administrative successor, in the name of Pope Gregory IX, received a piece of land from Simone Pucciarelli, on which to build a fitting oratory for the blessed body of the holy man. The land which was offered was the western slope of Mount Subasio. At the time, this hill was known locally as the "Hill of Hell," most probably because of its association as a place of public execution.

Pope Gregory IX laid the corner stone for the church on 17 July 1228, the day after the solemn canonization. On 22 April 1230 (fittingly, the eventual death anniversary of Brother Elias, the architect of the basilica), the "the Hill of Hell" was more appropriately renamed "the Hill of Paradise." On 25 May 1230, the body of the saint was transferred from his temporary resting place to the newly built church.

It is the common belief that because of the date on the first bell hung in the tower, the whole structure was completed within eleven years of its initiation, by 1239. Work then commenced on the interior decoration of frescoes and stained glass. The basilica was officially dedicated by Pope Innocent IV on 24 May 1253.

Naturally, any Franciscan or lover of the Franciscan story would admit that Francis himself probably would have been embarrassed by all the personal attention and fuss regarding such a beautiful church built in his honour. But a church, we must remember, although initiated in memorial to a particular person was an act of communal religious and civic pride, in this case, a gift of pink and white stone offered for the pleasure and worship of our future generations. A church was built in gratitude and praise to God. The basilica of Saint Francis was also understood as a centre of pilgrimage for people visiting from all over Europe and eventually the world. It was/is a genius of a classroom, offering not only evangelical instruction but hope to a weary world.

THE LOWER BASILICA
The Pilgrim Begins a Journey

The architecture of the lower basilica is romanesque in design. Romanesque is characterized by the rounded arch, low ceilings, thick walls and small windows. Romanesque architecture is a darker more enclosed environment than the later invention of gothic (the design of the upper basilica). The romanesque envelopes us in the peace and mystery of God, as if transporting us backward in time to the womb or forward in time to the tomb. The romanesque darkness calls for meditation on the life and death of Christ, the life and the death of the saint to which the church is dedicated.

The major art form of the basilica is fresco. Frescoes were sometimes called "the poor man's art," meaning they were intended as a passageway into profound simplicity, a communication with the Divine which all people could read. The Middle Ages were a time when theology was poetry; when theologians were not just professors of universities, but peasants, farmers and shop keepers; when the genius of a faithful soul united to a talented, artistic hand encouraged almost effortless communication with mystery itself. For the people of Francis' time, brush and canvas, hammer and chisel were the doorways of perception.

Thus poised for catechetical enchantment, the visitor enters the lower basilica and is welcomed by Francis himself, frescoed at the top of the first arch. The Latin inscription proclaims, *"Slow down your step and be joyful, oh pilgrim, you have already reached the hill of paradise... Ever resonant with praise and gladdened with holy choirs, this church is a true paradise of spiritual joys. Enter, you will see greater things."*

On the right side of the nave in the lower church, a staircase descends to the Tomb Chapel of Saint Francis. The pilgrim could either visit Francis' place of burial at the start of our journey or at the conclusion.

Originally, Francis' sacred remains were buried several meters under the high altar of the lower church. It was the common, if not a somewhat superstitious belief, that the more holy relics a town acquired (by whatever means, not excluding theft), then that town's prayers would be answered, battles won, economy improved. Thus, for practical reasons of security, the tomb of Saint Francis remained virtually out of public sight until the year 1818. At that time saint robbing was no longer a concern and Pope Pius VII gave permission for a beautiful crypt chapel to be constructed beneath the lower basilica so that all could at least gaze upon the stone sarcophagus, clearly visible in a hollowed out niche directly above the altar. In 1932 the Tomb Chapel was redesigned into the simple and austere sanctuary which we see today.

In all religions, death was a thing of great mystery and often accompanied by fear of the unknown afterlife. With the death and resurrection of Jesus Christ, Christians are assured that they will have many good companions for their journey into the beyond - the Son of God himself and the saints, our spiritual ancestors. Visiting the place of burial of any given saint is an act of sacred remembrance, an acknowledgement that we are a community of believers. We seek God as a family of faith.

In Assisi, the sepulchral church of Saint Francis concretely reminds us that we are one family in the Lord in that Francis is not alone in his tomb. Saint Francis is probably the first saint whose friends we know, four of whom are buried in the corners of the Tomb Chapel beside him: Masseo, "the handsome and eloquent nobleman filled with natural good sense"; Rufino, "the shy and prayerful" nobleman and cousin of Saint Clare; Leone, Francis' confessor and secretary, who together with the courteous Angelo, another noble knight, nursed Francis in his final days. These men were not Francis' religious subjects. His followers were his friends before and after his conversion. They followed Francis as a playboy soldier and they followed him as a committed religious founder. These followers were inspired by Christ and the Gospel teachings, but they were also inspired by the Christ they found in their friend.

THE NAVE

Jerusalem and Assisi

Artist: The Master of Saint Francis (c. 1236-?)

Moving forward and standing in the vestibule at the

entrance to the nave of the lower basilica, looking toward the altar, we find that we are surrounded by two series of frescoes, the harmony of *chronology and theme*. The frescoes on the right side of the nave represent the "passion" of Christ whereas the frescoes on the left, the mirror image, represent corresponding episodes of Francis' "compassion." The life of Francis is being offered as a role model *in vestigia Christi*, "robed in the person of Christ."

Unfortunately, around the year 1300 A.D., a brief sixty years after the completion of the basilica (1239), because of the multitude of pilgrims visiting the tomb of the new saint, it was decided to enlarge the lower basilica. Archways were constructed in the thick walls of the nave as grand portals for the addition of side chapels. But even though part of the story is missing, a spiritual meditation on the importance of the nave series would be well worth the pilgrim's patience, reconstructing the story with imagination.

The first fresco we see on the right wall of the nave is Christ being stripped of his clothing. (Although Christ can no longer be seen, remnants of his stripped garments are visible.) In Saint John's Gospel, Jesus, the "Son of God," is portrayed in control of his destiny, no one takes his life from him, he lays it down freely. But as the "Son of Man," possessed of finite human knowledge, even Jesus himself may not have understood the outcome of his obedience to the will of his Heavenly Father. Here Jesus shows himself as a man of trust and confidence. The removal of the exterior garments is the sign of his interior trust.

In the mirror fresco on the left wall of the nave, Francis has freely chosen to strip himself naked before his father and Bishop Guido of Assisi as a sign of his rejection of the suffocating social conformity. In imitation of Christ, Francis, a new man, borne of compassion, can also remove his exterior garments to show his interior conversion.

Moving to the third fresco on the right wall, we see Christ being taken down from the cross. To a rational person, this scene of the deceased Christ appears to be the end of the story. All the disciples have run off in fear. There will be no one to preach the Gospel message. Jesus is presented as a failure - as the world would account success and failure. But in the mirror fresco on the left we see one of the most famous depictions of Francis preaching to the birds. All of creation is rejoicing that the preaching of the Gospel has not died with the tragedy of the cross, but rather it has been spread to all parts of the world by new and courageous baptized followers. Heaven and earth are reconciled through the paradoxical life-giving cross of Christ (2 Cor. 5.18). The poor man of Assisi who, like every Christian, participates through baptism in the very life of Christ and reconciled through the blood of the Lamb, becomes a minister of that same reconciliation for all creation.

One final meditation in the *Master of Saint Francis* series calls for our attention to look upward. In the ceiling of the basilica we are struck by the richness of blue and the multitude of golden stars, each at one time having actual mirrors in their centre. The ceiling of the nave is the bridge between the life of Christ and the life of Francis. Heaven, so to speak, has been captured on earth. The lessons of the Bible and the lessons of our heroes, the saints, are not to be left in the past, they are meant for now. The Kingdom of God is a present reality.

THE CROSS VAULTING ABOVE THE ALTAR
The Evangelical Virtues: Poverty, Chastity, Obedience
Artist: The Master of the Vele (c. 1320-?)

The nave series of frescoes, presenting Francis as a model disciple, fittingly propels us toward the altar, the centre or focus of the entire building, the place where the sacred mysteries are celebrated. The sacraments of the altar are the meeting place of time and eternity, of heaven and earth, of God and creation. It is in the heart of the church, gathered around the table of nourishment, sacrifice, praise, fraternity, mission that we are able to shout with our ancestors of centuries past, *"Amen, Yes, Lord, we believe!"*

It is not surprising therefore, that in this central culmination point that we should encounter a particular density of the art form through which we are given an entrance into the very soul of Francis of Assisi.

For Francis there were two "windows" through which he could gaze upon the life of Jesus and inevitably into the very essence of the life of God. The first "window" was the Incarnation, the birth of God in human form (Phil. 2:6-7), clearly depicted in the frescoes in the right transept, the Infancy cycle of Christ. The second "window" through which Francis would enter in communion with the God of Love is shown in the total abandonment of the Son to the will of the Father as modelled in the left transept, the Passion and Death cycle of Christ (Heb. 5:8-9).

The means by which Francis could enter these "windows" and unite himself to the Beloved in the Incarnation and Passion was through an intensification of his baptismal commitment. Looking upward at the four allegorical panels frescoed directly over the high altar the pilgrim will see every Christian's clearly charted course to the Father - as interpreted through the Franciscan perspective - the often misinterpreted evangelical virtues: Poverty, Chastity and Obedience.

It is also significant that the scenes of these allegorical virtues are set atop a mountain. The high places are evocative of the Old Testament encounters with God, especially that of Moses on Mount Sinai, where he was given the Ten Commandments, the Torah. Another account of a mountain experience was the New Testament story of the Transfiguration on Mount Tabor. We are given a glimpse of that glory, lost through Adam's disobedience, now restored to humanity through the sacrifice of Christ. It is precisely over the altar, the place of celebrating the heavenly mysteries, that we too are bathed in Taboric light; we have died and are risen with Christ, we have been given a new Law, we are made into a "new creation." That the *allegories* are all set against a gold background, as compared to the blue background in the right and left transepts, calls to mind the in-breaking of Divine glory into our world of time and space. No longer is the following of the letter of the Law the path to God, but we must write the Law in our hearts (Rom. 7:1-25). In so doing our lives will be transfigured and will become faithful examples for an anxious world.

In Renaissance art, virtues are portrayed as knightly, courtly images very much in keeping with Francis' ideal of chivalry. Thus, each virtue is personified as: Lady Obedience, Lady Poverty and Lady Chastity.

Lady Obedience is seated in front of Saint Francis who is kneeling. She is placing a yoke over his neck. A yoke, the symbol of responsibility, is not being forced on Francis. He is reaching up freely and taking the yoke on his own shoulders. The word obedience derives from the Latin, literally meaning "listen." Lady Obedience is shown with her fingers up to her lips in the gesture of instruction, "Be quiet and listen;" listen to the will of God, listen to the needs of others and listen to your own needs. Two virtues accompany us on our journey toward an obedient, listening life style: Lady Humility, on the right of Obedience, with her head bowed, carrying a candle of self-knowledge, and Lady Prudence on the left, exposing two faces. Lady Prudence has an older, more mature face looking back to her past because she is aware of her ancestry, she is not forsaking her past, she has learned from it. Lady Prudence is looking forward into a mirror because she knows who she is today, she is not self-deceived. She has turned the mirror around to face Francis - symbolizing the main character's sense of introspection. The right hand of Lady Prudence holds mathematical instruments of calculation because she is charting her future. Therefore, Lady Prudence teaches us that we can never truly be an obedient person, or rather, we can never listen to the will of God or the needs of others or our own needs, if we are not a *whole person*; if we do not know our past, if we do not know who we are today, if we do not have some direction for the future.

In the right section of the Obedience allegory we can see an angel casting out Pride. He is half man, half beast - a centaur - an adaption from ancient Greek mythology, a deformed being. The negative aspect of pride, selfishness, deforms our human nature. Pride is so full of himself that he cannot hear the needs of others. His punishment is to be cast out so as not to infect the serious seeker of truth.

In the upper section of the Obedience allegory, we see Saint Francis being drawn up into heaven by the yoke of responsibility still around his neck. But if we look closer, we realize that there are no strings attached between the hands of God and the shoulders of Francis. Francis is not being manipulated like a marionette. He freely chooses to serve the will of God because he knows that only in freedom can love exist.

Lady Chastity, far from being a caricature of sexual abstention, teaches the pilgrim that this most often misinterpreted virtue is the integration of all the creative and life-communicating energies of a human person. Lady Chastity is like the athlete of old, sacrificing herself for a higher goal, the achievement of greater competitive physical endurance, testing her will, purifying her intentions, strengthening her focus.

Lady Chastity is seated in a tower surrounded by two beautiful angels; one bringing the crown of salvation, the other a palm tree of victory. The white flag of purity and self-surrender waves boldly atop the tower.

Below can be seen two angels ritually bathing a

young man as part of the ceremony of knighthood. A knight was not just a soldier. Any peasant could have been made a soldier at the whim of the local lord. A knight was an advancement into the ruling class. A knight was a man who wanted to live by a code of honour, to serve and protect the weak of society. To be a knight was the greatest goal of Francis' early life. Thus, after his conversion he chooses to adapt the ideals of knighthood and chivalry into the lifestyle of a wandering religious. It is because of his choice of selfless service that two other angels are about to robe Francis - the actual knighthood candidate - in the rose coloured garments of wisdom.

The two virtues which assist Francis as dutiful knight errants are reaching their hands over the castle walls offering the aid of a lance and shield, his new armour for an interior battle, which are of course, their identities: Munificence - purity, graciousness - and Fortitude, strength. The knight is recognized as an "officer and a gentleman," we would say nowadays.

In the section on the right of the Chastity allegory we find triplets, Faith, Hope and Charity, accompanied by their friend, Penance. These virtues are casting out the evil spirits that are opposing a chaste lifestyle. The spirit with a quiver of arrows and a string of hearts around his chest is the most interesting. He is the pagan god of love, Cupid or Eros. In this scene Cupid is blindfolded, representing that he has not made a lasting commitment to the wholeness of another. The god Cupid lives only for momentary physical pleasure. The true God of Love is faithful, focused. The true follower of the Christian God of Love, is not concerned only with the physical aspect of another person but can see and can love them as a whole person, on good days as well as bad, in richness and in poverty, in sickness and in health.

The marriage of Saint Francis to Lady Poverty is the central focus of the third allegory. Francis is placing a ring on her finger while Christ stands between them blessing the marriage. On the right of Lady Poverty are the two witnesses of the marriage, the two virtues who will accompany the bridal couple throughout their lives, Lady Hope, wearing green, the bearer of the ring, and Lady Charity, wearing a rose coloured garment and holding a heart in her hand.

What at first resembles two small boys in the foreground are in reality two grown men. Their smallness of stature represents their distance from the scene. There is a great canyon separating them from the main characters. These two men in red and blue represent the merchant class, the rising monied class of the time. Francis was part of this new monied class. But after his conversion Francis always had a great fear that money could lead people to depend more on themselves rather than on God, rather than on their neighbour. Thus, these two men are throwing stones or poking thorn branches at Lady Poverty, casting her out. They are saying "We don't need you. We don't need to depend on anyone else. We are self-sufficient in our coinage." But every story we read in the scriptures teaches us that God can always take our misdirections and redirect them toward a good outcome. Through patience and perseverance, our sacrifices, mirrored in the brambles at the base of Lady Poverty's feet, eventually blossom into a rose bush of blessings crowning her head.

The angel on the lower left of the Poverty allegory is offering this virtue of poverty/simplicity to the rich young Francis who is shown giving away his clothing to a poor man. The angel in the upper left section of the scene is taking the good deed, in the form of the red cape, up to the hands of God. Whenever we give to the poor it is like giving to God. Another angel is bringing along a house with a large walled vegetable garden. Hence, the three basic needs are represented: food, shelter and clothing. We are all called to take care of the needs of those less fortunate than ourselves.

On the vice side of the Poverty allegory, we have another angel trying to encourage three men to give up something for the betterment of the community, but they are refusing. Interestingly, these three men also represent a social commentary on the Feudal system. The man closest to the angel is a nobleman having a falcon on his arm, representing the sport of hunting. Power is in the hands of a few and he is refusing to share it. The man on the far end, representing the rising merchant class, is clutching a money bag to his chest. The economy is in the hands of a few and he is refusing to share it. The man in the middle, who has completely turned his gaze away from the scene, is clutching a book to his chest, representing culture and learning as being in the hands of a few. This man is a member of the clergy. He is tonsured. Oddly enough, the artist seems to be criticizing the clergy even though he was working for the Pope. However, since this art work had to be approved by the official Church before it ever went on to the walls, the Church itself, as the commissioning institution, really did not spare anyone, not even itself. The clear message is that we are all called to live as simply as possible no matter who we are. We are all called to live so that our possessions do not come to possess us.

FRANCIS IN GLORY

If we try to live these three virtues in our lives: Obedience, a listening life style; Chastity, a faithful life-style; Poverty, a simple life style, then we will be assured of heaven. If then, the viewer looks upward at the allegorical scene located above the choir stalls one will see Saint Francis in glory. Naturally, during his life time Francis was a man of the poor and simple, he never wore a habit of gold. This scene however, depicts Francis after his death, robed in heavenly glory, a glory which will also be ours. Francis holds a book of the Gospels as an orb and a cross as a septre. He is seated on a throne surrounded by angels who are singing, dancing and playing musical instruments, calling all of us into heavenly glory as well.

THE SPIRITUALITY OF ARCHITECTURE

A further appreciation of the allegories of the virtues is understood when learning that the artist is only referred to as the *Master of the Vele*. *"Vele"*, in Italian, translates into "sails," which alludes to the triangular shapes of the vaulting resembling the sails of a ship. The medieval pilgrim would have been aware that the very architecture itself was also intended as instructive.

Looking upward at the vaulting in the nave, a word deriving from the Latin, *navis*, a "ship," we are reminded of the traditional image of the Church as a community of believers journeying toward God as if on the deck of a great sailing vessel. As long as we are on board we are safe from the waters of the storm-tossed sea of false values which threaten to destroy us.

While sailing toward God, the priest, our presider,

is our captain guiding the community from the helm, the altar, the place of worship. The pulpit is the navigation desk where our course is charted through the preaching of the scriptures. The method by which any ship continues its movement toward a safe harbour is by keeping wind in the sails. Thus, behind the altar, in the prow, is the source of our wind power, the prayer which rises from the choir stalls. Much like the steady and precise rowing of oars, the daily prayers of the religious community are chanted in a back and forth movement between the right and the left side of the choir. As God the Father created the first human being by sharing his breath we continue to share life with our fellow pilgrims by sharing our breath, sharing our prayer. It is this shared, steady breathing in the act of public and private worship which gives wind to our sails and carries us forward. While sitting in the choir for the resident friars or sitting in the nave for the traveling pilgrims, we are all focused on our destination by the expansion of the wind in the sails above the altar, the *vele*, the evangelical virtues, our path to God. If ever we stop praying, the wind in the sails dies. Our life directions cease movement and the ship, the whole community of believers, is weakened.

THE RIGHT TRANSEPT
The Infancy of Christ
Artist: Giotto (c. 1309-?)

The genius of the Franciscan movement in the early thirteenth century was that it reminded people that God created the world good. In fact, the world was so good that one could see the face of God in God's own creation; in the beauty of a sunset, in trees and flowers, even in the physical form of another person, a neighbour. Francis' great desire then, and what becomes the "Franciscan revolution," is this bold attempt to *rehumanize* God - the desire to bring what was perceived as a distant God back into the ordinary lives of ordinary people. To accomplish this task Francis sends his *friars* (from the Latin, meaning "brothers") into the busyness and messiness of the marketplace, into the buying and the selling of the town square, or into the fields to work among the labourers. The friars soon become known as the "Jugglers of God" because of the dramatic spectacle they create by dancing, singing, performing acrobatics. Attracting large crowds they preach the Gospel message in a new way - a joyful way. All of a sudden God is in the midst of ordinary people, sharing their joys and sorrows as are these poor mendicants, these wandering troubadours of the Most High King.

Thus, the art of this basilica profoundly teaches the Gospel message from the Franciscan point of view, a renewed vision, a renewed hope.

Even if the viewer has seen Renaissance art before visiting Assisi, what is important to remember is that for the first time in Europe - about 1296, in Assisi - a person could walk into this church, gaze upward, and not only see a holy person but they would have also seen a tree, or flowers on a balcony, or a landscape - as in the Visitation episode. For the first time in art, the Nativity scene presents ordinary farm animals, reverently poised and breathing on the Christ Child. In the same Nativity scene, shepherds are being spoken to by angels. Shepherds are poor people. The lower classes were never portrayed in art before this time. In the Adoring Magi panel, Mary is presenting Christ to three Wise Men who are dressed like Medieval nobility from Florence. Mary is seated in a stable that looks like an Italian villa. In the Presentation panel, Mary and Joseph are offering their child for a blessing in the Temple of Jerusalem which looks remarkably like the upper basilica.

What is being communicated to the pilgrim for the first time in art, in a very powerfully symbolic way, is

that God is born in Italy - God is born in Assisi, Italy, *today*. God is not only born so many hundreds of years ago in Bethlehem, Israel. God is alive and well in our present generation.

Remaining in this transept and continuing the theme of the rehumanization-of-the-divine, we could turn our gaze to the crucifixion. And even though we have all seen crucifixions before arriving in Assisi, what is important to remember here is that this scene is credited with being the first time holy people express emotion in art.

Prior to the artist Giotto, if one saw a crucifixion, Christ would have been portrayed in the traditional byzantine fashion, very stylized, showing no human emotion whatsoever. Again, up until the time of Francis, the mentality for centuries was that Christ, as a divine personage, could not suffer like an ordinary human being. In the previous style of art the crucified Jesus would also have been dressed in the robes of a priest or a king. Here in Assisi, in this transept, for the first time in art, we see a God who has suffered and died. He is not just pretending to die on the cross, as many heresies of the Middle Ages believed. Christ has black marks on his chest where he has been beaten. His head is bowed. His eyes are closed. He is immodestly dressed. He is profusely bleeding into a bowl which an angel is trying to keep from spilling on the ground.

The angels in this crucifixion scene, spiritual beings who are always in the presence of God and who should behave with greater foresight, are also showing messy human emotion for the first time in art. The angel who is catching the blood from the side of Christ is turning its face away, he cannot even look upon what humanity has done to the Son of God. One of the angels on the right is scratching his cheeks with his fingernails, drawing blood. The angel next to him is rending his garments, exposing his chest. The Medieval pilgrim gazing at these images would have naturally recognized these symbols of grief and despair but they would have never before associated them with angels. In the lower left hand corner, Mary, the Mother of Christ, has also fainted from grief and despair. This seems like a rather normal human emotion for the modern viewer, after all her son has just been crucified. But for the Medieval viewer, their religious sensitivities would have been trained to see the Virgin Mary in complete control of her emotions. She is the Queen of heaven and earth, always very much aware that her son is God. The new perspective of the Franciscan movement, first enfleshed by the Florentine artist Giotto, offers great comfort to a people who were sending their sons, fathers, brothers or husbands into battle and not knowing if they were coming back alive. How comforting for people to know that the Mother of God, the Son of God and the angels themselves, were sharing all of their messy human emotions. It was a renewed idea that made life valuable - God shares in my life and I share in the life of God.

As mentioned, colours also played an important role in the presentation of lessons within lessons. Therefore, another insight into the same crucifixion scene comes from the colour of the Virgin Mary's garment. Traditionally, Mary wears blue, the strict byzantine convention representing divinity or heavenly status. In this depiction the fainted Queen of heaven is wearing a rose coloured gown, representing wisdom. Mary is depicted being clothed in wisdom because she knows there is more to the story than this present moment of despair, there will be a reunion of the Beloved in heaven. All will be well.

THE LEFT TRANSEPT
The Passion and Death of Christ
Artists: Pietro and Ambrogio Lorenzetti (c. 1320-?)

An often visited small corner of the basilica brings us to the fresco just below the crucifixion scene, that of the Madonna and Child. The infant Jesus is shown whispering to his mother, "Which one should I bless, John the Apostle or Saint Francis?" The Blessed Mother discreetly points to Saint Francis. With this scene the artists were not trying to upstage Christ or John the Apostle, rather, they were holding up Francis as a role model, a "new apostle," a man whose life vision was confirmed

by the stigmata, the sharing of the wounds of Christ (as will be explained later in the text). A further *highlight* of this fresco is enjoyed if the pilgrim is fortunate enough to view the setting summer sun mystically illuminating the exact dimensions of the episode. Hence, the more common and affectionate title, *Our Lady of the Sunset*.

Although the art of this transept is rich in detail, we will focus on just one *often missed* facet of the despair-hope theme in this Passion and Death cycle.

Hidden in the darkness on the left of the staircase is the Apostle Judas hanging himself. After the crucifixion, the suicide of Judas was a recurrent theme in sermons of the time. The Judas story reminds all Christians that threat of divine punishment was a common form of inducing individuals or societies into good behaviour. The Franciscans, having a more positive outlook on the mercy of God, manipulated this common moral into something less intimidating.

In the opposite transept (the Giotto Infancy cycle), in the exact location beside the staircase we discover that

this desperate suicidal presentation is only half of the story.

Walking into the Giotto transept again, looking at the right of the staircase, we see Francis standing beside a skeleton, his left hand tenderly on its shoulder, his stigmatized hand beckoning us forward. The skeleton, representing death, is wearing a golden crown, representing power. But the crown is falling off the head of the skeleton. Through the resurrection, death has lost its power over us. Not only has death been conquered but Francis is welcoming us into death. Death for him is no longer an end, but a doorway into a deeper relationship with God. Francis, a man who poetically personified nature, *brother sun, sister moon, brother wind, sister water*, also calls death a "sister." As Judas hung himself because he did not believe in the pardon of God, Saint Francis opened himself to grace in imitation of the unfathomable forgiveness of the cross.

Such an episodial coupling - Judas on the left with Sister Death on the right - stories frescoed by different artists in different decades, again offers us an insight into the art work of the basilica as a single strategy of theology, "a calculated trap for meditation".

With the conclusion of our meditations in the lower basilica, the pilgrim could proceed up the stairs to the outside courtyard where another set of stairs will take you to the upper basilica.

THE UPPER BASILICA
Salvation History

The transepts and apse: Cimabue and the School of Rome (c. 1280-?)
The nave: Giotto (c. 1296-?)

Both upper and lower basilicas actually form one single construction. Together they lead the pilgrim on a double journey. The lower romanesque church, dark and womb-like, leads us in meditation to the heart, to the silent centre of our being. The splendid luminosity of the upper gothic church naturally lifts our eyes and spirits upward following the graceful lines of the pillars ascending toward heaven like an avenue of perfect *Trees of Life* in a renewed paradise. Creation has been reborn in the realization that our God acts in the dynamic flow of history, we are not left abandoned. This renewed relationship leads us on an outward journey, on mission, to the very limits of our humanity.

The whole edifice of this upper church, like the whole historical process, is focused in the central ceiling area of the nave, in the depiction of Christ in Majesty. The Master Teacher is the *alpha* and *omega*, the beginning and the end (Rev. 21:6). The three rondels surrounding Christ offer witnesses of a life on high. On the mirror side of Christ is Saint Francis, faithful follower and emulator of the Gospel. John the Baptist, the last archetypal Old Testament prophet, is seen on Christ's left

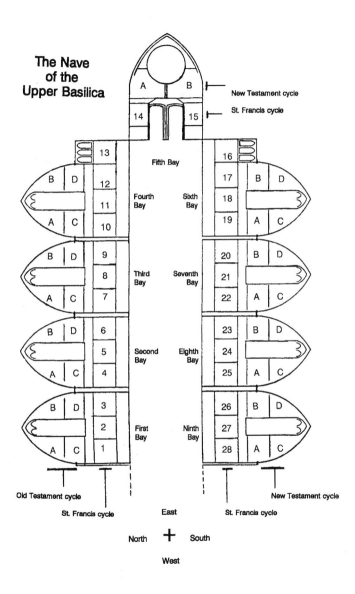

The Nave
of the
Upper Basilica

New Testament cycle

St. Francis cycle

A   B

14   15

13   Fifth Bay   16

B D   17

12   Fourth   Sixth   18   B D

11   Bay   Bay   19

A C   10   A C

B D   9   20   B D

8   Third   Seventh   21

A C   7   Bay   Bay   22   A C

B D   6   23   B D

5   Second   Eighth   24

A C   4   Bay   Bay   25   A C

B D   3   26   B D

2   First   Ninth   27

A C   1   Bay   Bay   28   A C

Old Testament cycle

St. Francis cycle

New Testament cycle

St. Francis cycle

East

North ✛ South

West

OLD TESTAMENT

I-A   Creation
I-B   Creation of Man
I-C   Building the Ark
I-D   The Ark sailing
II-A   Creation of Woman
II-B   The Fall
II-C   Abraham's Sacrifice
II-D   Abraham with angels
III-A   Expulsion from Eden
III-B   Adam & Eve labouring
III-C   Isaac and Jacob
III-D   Isaac and Esau
IV-A   Cain and Abel
IV-B   Cain killing Abel
IV-C   Joseph sold
IV-D   Joseph in Egypt

NEW TESTAMENT

V-A   Pentecost
V-B   Ascension
VI-A   Lamentation of women
VI-B   After Resurrection
VI-C   Teaching in Temple
VI-D   Baptism of Christ
VII-A   Way of the Cross
VII-B   Crucifixion
VII-C   Presentation in Temple
VII-D   Flight into Egypt
VIII-A Betrayal of Judas
VIII-B Scourging
VIII-C Nativity
VIII-D Visit of Magi
IX-A   Feast at Cana
IX-B   Lazarus
IX-C   Annunciation

IX-D   Visitation

LEGEND OF FRANCIS

I-1   Francis honoured
I-2   Offering his cloak
I-3   Vision of armour
II-4   Vision in San Damiano
II-5   Renunciation of clothes
II-6   Vision of Innocent III
III-7   Confirmation of Rule
III-8   Vision of fiery chariot
III-9   Vision of Thrones
IV-10   Evil in Arezzo
IV-11   Before the Sultan
IV-12   Francis in ecstasy
IV-13   Christmas at Greccio
V-14   Miracle of the water
V-15   Sermon to the birds
VI-16   Knight of Celano
VI-17   Before Honorius III
VI-18   Vision of St. Anthony
VI-19   Receiving the stigmata
VII-20 Death of Francis
VII-21 Vision of Br Agostino
VII-22 Verification of stigmata
VIII-23 Mourning of Clares
VIII-24 Canonization of Francis
VIII-25 Vision of Gregory IX
IX-26   Miracle: physical healing
IX-27   Miracle: spiritual healing
IX-28   Miracle: healed reputation

where the presentation of the Genesis covenant promises are frescoed on the upper most registers of the left walls. The Virgin Mary is honoured on Christ's right. Because of her faithfulness to the will of God she is the heraldress of the New Testament, as frescoed on the upper most registers of the right walls.

The two large crucifixions located on the East walls of the transepts comfort the pilgrim to know that God the Father judges us through rose coloured glasses, through the eyes of his Son in the perfect act of obedience. Through the paradox of the cross sinful humanity has been redeemed. We have the possibility, the unimaginable possibility of living forever in the presence of God.

If looking toward the rose window, we turn our gaze toward the end walls of the left transept (although almost completely faded), we see the scriptural episodes of the Acts of the Apostles. The Book of the Apocalypse, the last book of the Bible, is frescoed in the right transept. The beginning of the Church as recounted in the Acts of the Apostles and the Church continuing into the future in the Book of the Apocalypse envelopes the pilgrim in a secure plan of salvation.

The whole scriptural synthesis is concluded on either side of the beautiful rose window, which is itself a symbol of the risen Christ, the rudder of our spiritual ship, the "Eye of God" watching over his followers. The rays of the rose window fan outward from the flaming concentrated centre, bathing all of creation, the cosmos, in his peaceful yet glorious light. To the right of the window is seen the Ascension of Christ to the Father. To the left of the window is the descent of the Holy Spirit on the apostles gathered in the upper room at Pentecost. We are left with the trust that we are not orphaned, Christ will be with us even until the end of the world.

Having situated the scriptures as our primary source of inspiration in the upper registers of the walls, we are now prepared to trace our way through the complementary episodes in the life of Francis of Assisi as frescoed in the encircling panels on the lower registers of the nave.

THE NAVE
The Life of Saint Francis
Artist: Giotto (c. 1296-?)

The Life of Saint Francis, as frescoed by the great artist Giotto in the upper basilica, is based on the *Legenda Major* written by Saint Bonaventure in 1263, at least three decades before Giotto begins to paint. A *legenda* in this instance refers to a type of story which was divided into thematic chapters for purposes of instruction. Each window bay of the basilica is the unfolding of several theological or catechetical subjects particular in the lives of both Christ and Saint Francis, and ultimately, in the lives of us all.

THE FIRST WINDOW BAY
Francis, Man of Conversion

Francis was born in the year 1182. He died in 1226. In the first episode [I-1] Francis is shown as a young man, about twenty years old. The Temple of Minerva is clearly recognizable in the town square. A man of common origin is spreading his cape over a puddle of water as a sign of honour and respect. The man makes a prophesy: "One day you will do great things." Francis simply believes he will do great things in battle, eventually earning recognition for valour and receiving the honour of knighthood.

The biographies tell us that Francis had lived a wild and frivolous life up until this time. Although not nobility, Francis was quite wealthy. His father was an industrious cloth merchant, part of the new rising middle class, who indulged the boy in everything. Because of his delight in singing the songs of the French troubadours, Francis' friends dub him the "king of song."

Because the life cycle of Saint Francis, as frescoed in this basilica, is considered the first time that a "real" scene is depicted, rather than just "stylized" buildings, any pilgrim of the Middle Ages visiting Assisi would have known that the Temple of Minerva was used as a court room and prison. The reason the Temple-prison is taking predominance as the central focus of the scene is precisely because Francis is imprisoned in himself, in his selfishness. But if the viewer looks at the pediment of the Temple a rose window can be seen. Because there has never been a rose window on the pediment of the Temple of Minerva the Medieval pilgrim, accustomed to symbolic juxtapositions, would have probably understood that the rose window, representing the "Eye of God" watching over his creation, is also watching over Francis, even though Francis is not even aware of it. It is only through the power of God that Francis breaks out of the prison of selfishness and can begin his earthly conversion.

The second episode [I-2] occurs a little more than one year after the first. Fighting against Perugia, the mortal enemy of Assisi, Francis is captured in battle and is thrown into a damp, dark dungeon as a prisoner of war. Even though he tried to maintain the morale of his fellow prisoners Francis eventually succumbed to illness and depression. In episode two, we see Francis after his release from prison. While riding through the countryside he encounters a poorly dressed knight. Francis is so moved by the knight's shabby appearance that he offers the man his own fine clothing.

For a modern audience the offering of a cape to a poorly dressed soldier may not be immediately understandable. Remember, this was an age of chivalry. As mentioned in the allegory of Chastity in the lower basilica, the knight was not only a man who defended a city during time of war, he was a person vowed to a code of honour. He held a position of dignity and leadership within the civic community. Francis' act of generosity is also reminiscent of another encounter with a leper. This meeting of the poor knight is extremely similar in its presentation. Francis, a handsome young man, at one time nauseated by the sight of lepers, a disease thought to be highly contagious, offered his clothing and the kiss of peace to a leper whom he happened to meet on a country road. Francis, who freely disrobes himself several times: before the knight, the leper and his father [II-5], is being presented as an example of taking off the old man and putting on the new.

In the third episode [I-3] all of Francis' high ideals and former resolutions fade away when another crusade is called. Again, he is captivated by the thought of exterior glory and honour and rushes off to enlist. The night before the battle Christ appears to Francis in a dream. Christ offers a castle filled with red and white armour, telling Francis to choose between the master or the servant. Francis tells the Lord he would rather serve the master. Christ tells Francis to return home. Francis, already a proven warrior in battle, does as the dream-vision commands. He returns home and is ridiculed by his fellow townspeople as a coward.

If the viewer will stand back to look up into the Old Testament cycle above the Francis episodes, you will see God creating the world as recorded in the Book of Genesis [I-A] and God creating Adam [I-B]. Below that is Noah being commissioned [I-C] and sailing for forty days in the ark [I-D]. Francis' life is intricately linked to the themes of the scriptures above. As with the creation of Adam, Francis is reborn when meeting Christ through charity offered to a poor knight and a leper. Like Noah, Francis shows himself a man willing to begin again. Even in his confusion, Francis remains loyal to the dream-vision. He never picks up the sword again.

THE SECOND WINDOW BAY
Francis, Man of Trust

Episode four [II-4] finds Francis seeking refuge far from his angry parents and his mocking friends. It is in the silence and darkness of the dilapidated church of San Damiano where he can finally be alone with his thoughts.

The crucifix hanging in the church, known as the cross of San Damiano, is a whole text book of theology in itself. And it was during those soul wrenching days after obedience to the dream-vision when Francis finally heard the Christ of the San Damiano cross speaking so clearly: "Go and repair my house, for as you can see it is falling into ruin." Whether Francis heard the words of Christ through his ears or through his heart, it really does not matter. What is important is that he takes action. Francis goes to Foligno, another nearby town, to sell several bolts of his father's cloth to buy stones to rebuild San Damiano. Francis even sells his horse. Again, for the modern audience one must remember what selling a horse signified for the Middle Ages. A horse was not only a means of transportation, a horse was a battle animal. This is the point of no return. Francis is giving up the opportunity for glory in battle. He is also refusing to help defend his town from its enemies, a matter of obligation for his class. On his way back to Assisi, Francis meets another poor man on the road. He exchanges his rich clothing and steps out of his class for ever. Francis makes himself a peasant, albeit a poetic one, an ordinary labourer, or worse, a beggar.

In episode five [II-5] Francis stands before his father in the court of Bishop Guido of Assisi. Francis' father, Pietro di Bernardone, was a materialistic man, to say the least, but we must not judge him too harshly. Pietro, like any parent, had been patient for as long as possible, two years in fact, with all of the goings and comings of his son. But finally Pietro's anger unleashes its full wrath. Pietro wants restitution for all the cloth which Francis has sold or given away which was not his right to do. The biographies attest that Francis was sincerely afraid of his father and often shows him hiding until this ultimate moment of renunciation.

In the presence of the bishop, his judge, Francis strips himself of all of his clothing, the last remnants of those things that belong to his father and hands them back. Although Bishop Guido robes Francis in his cape, a sign of taking Francis into the protection of the Church, this is still an extremely sad moment in the Franciscan story. We are not sure whether or not Francis ever reconciled with his father. Saint Bonaventure, the author of these events, is putting across to the audience that following the will of God is not always an easy road. Earthly values or materialism and pleasure do not compare with heavenly glory and heavenly virtues. But there is a price if one desires to live by Gospel values.

For two more years, as Francis wanders, begs and prays in quiet lonely places, several of his rich and noble friends, who were as carefree and as idealistic as he, finally come to appreciate his sincerity. Francis' new adventure is too seductive to resist. They join him. When the number of followers reaches twelve, Francis decides to go to Rome to seek approval for his growing community.

In episode six [II-6] we see Pope Innocent III receiving a dream-vision in Rome (1209). Although Innocent III was one of the greatest mystical and political minds of the Middle Ages, the Church had fallen into laxity and corruption.

In the dream-vision the Pope sees the mother church of Christianity, Saint John Lateran (the government centre) crumbling to the ground. Suddenly, a poorly dressed man appears holding up the entire structure on his shoulder. Pope Innocent believes this is the divine confirmation that someone will come to help him in reforming the crumbling Church. The next day Francis is presented. The Pope recognizes the beggar as the man in his dream the night before and gives Francis' community formal approval. The new community is called the Friars

Minor, from the Latin "lesser brothers."

It may also be noticed that Francis is holding the building up with his hand turned inward. Francis is trying to heal the institution from within rather than attack it from without.

If the viewer stands back to visualize the three Francis episodes in this second window bay as a whole one may notice the playful convention of using the angles of buildings or scenery to teach lessons within lessons. In episode six [II-6] the church of Saint John Lateran is crumbling to the ground, representing the corruption of the leadership. In episode four [II-4] the church of San Damiano, the church of the ordinary people, is also crumbling, representing the corruption of morals in the laity. Both churches have the same angled foundation because both buildings represent the same Church, as clergy, as laity. If your eyes follow the angles of the buildings upward you find that they meet in the clothing thrown over the arm of Francis' father in episode five [II-5]. Francis is again shown as a man of trust, able to see beyond the difficulties of the present moment. He can give away his exterior garments witnessing to his interior conversion. Together with Christ in Saint John's Gospel, Francis offers his life freely, no one takes it from him.

The central focus of episode five [II-5], Francis' intense gaze at the hand of God blessing him from the clouds, draws our attention even beyond, into the upper registers of the Old Testament series, a further reinforcement of this theme of trust. The upper most fresco on the left has God creating woman from the rib of Adam [II-A]. There is the trust that the species will continue. To the right [II-B] we see Adam and Eve being expelled from the Garden of Eden because of disobedience. And yet, the compassionate Creator has robed them in furs for protection. God punishes sin but he is always ready to offer mercy. The two episodes in the middle register have the Patriarch Abraham about to slay his son Isaac as a sign of trust in God's will [II-C]. Abraham is stopped from the deed by the hand of an angel telling him the request was only a test. Abraham's progeny will continue.

THE FOURTH WINDOW BAY
Francis, the Intercessor

Standing in front of the fourth window bay the famous Old Testament story of Joseph and his coat of many colours [IV-C,D] offers the theme that we are all called to be intercessors before God.

Joseph, the second youngest of the twelve sons of Jacob (the son of Isaac), is best loved by his aging father. Because of the jealousy of his brothers, Joseph is sold into slavery. Several adventures land Joseph in prison in Egypt. But because Joseph has the gift of interpreting dreams he wins Pharaoh's favour and saves the Egyptians and Hebrews from seven years of severe famine. As God could work reversals in Joseph's life so can he work reversals in our lives. It was through the paradox of an evil deed, being sold into slavery, that Joseph is eventually able to save his people from starvation years later.

Thus, the four episodes in Francis' life on the lower level so expertly match the themes of the Patriarch Joseph. The Francis episodes show the importance of beseeching heaven for all people in need. Francis is an intercessor between rich and poor Christians as when he was summoned to the town of Arezzo to cast out the evil in the hearts of the feuding classes [IV-10]. Francis intercedes between Christians and non-Christians as when he visits the Sultan of Egypt attempting to bring peace during the time of the Crusades [IV-11]. Francis intercedes between God and humanity through his own personal prayer by symbolically rising to God in ecstacy on a cloud [IV-12]. Francis intercedes between God and humanity by dramatizing the nativity scene in a cave near the town of Greccio two years before his death [IV-13].

The New Testament stories of Christ teaching in the Temple as a boy [VI-C], his baptism in the River Jordan by his cousin John [VI-D], the Lamentation of the women of Jerusalem while Christ carries his cross [VI-A] and the women present at the empty tomb after his resurrection [VI-B], all present Christ as the Master Teacher, model of obedience to the will of his Heavenly

Father.

Francis, exemplar of Christ, is portrayed in four episodes below the New Testament cycle as a man diligent in teaching various levels of society the true way of following the Gospel. In episode sixteen [VI-16] Francis, attending a meal with friends, prophesies that his host, the kindly Knight of Celano must make a quick confession because the Lord will take his life soon. In fact, the Knight dies during the meal. We are being reminded that we never know the day or the hour, we must be prepared to meet our Maker at any time. Episode seventeen [VI-17] has Francis preaching to the Papal court, men considered the most learned scholars of those days. In simplicity, Francis reminds these great men that words must be put into practice. Episode eighteen [VI-18] has Francis appearing in a dream-vision to Saint Anthony of Padua in the city of Arles, France, where Anthony, a learned scholar himself, had been commissioned to educate the friars. Francis cautions Anthony not to extinguish the spirit of prayer so that his brother friars will not become haughty through the attainment of privileged knowledge.

Episode nineteen [VI-19] is the stigmata. Two years before his death, just when everything seemed to be going wrong in his life, Francis receives a great gift. While praying in anguish on Mount La Verna, beseeching the heavens for an answer to the misdirections of his multitude of followers, Christ appears to Francis being carried by a six-winged angel, a seraph. Christ comforts Francis by telling him to trust again, and all will be well. Christ embraces Francis and leaves with him the imprint of the crucifixion. In this dramatic scene Francis is actually receiving his wish of knighthood, he is being dubbed by the Most High Liege Lord. Francis has proven himself a worthy knight errant and now shares in his Master's triumph, the battle scars of love. Interior nobility, Francis discovers, is a greater glory than exterior pomp.

Another level of meaning is discovered in this stigmata scene when realizing that what may at first appear as decorative weeds in the foreground are in fact herbs easily recognizable to the medieval agricultural society. The small plant having the single yellow flower is *tussilago farfara*, commonly known as the "Son before the Father." The flower of this herb has the unusual pattern of blossoming several months before the leaves sprout. The herb having brilliant blue star-shaped flowers is *borago officinalis* or borage. Having a great variety of medicinal qualities it was often used against the common cold. According to one ancient doctor, when borage was made into a wine "it drove away sadness and made men merry and joyful." Naturally, the symbolism of these two herbs appropriately intensifies the above story of the stigmata. Francis has come to know the Son, and through the Son he recognizes the Father. Although Francis suffered great physical agonies toward the end of his life he is forever remembered as a man of joy, able to "drive away the sadness" of those who had lost hope.

THE FIFTH WINDOW BAY
Francis, Man of Mission

The fifth window bay, clearly the conclusion in the overall cycle, directs us outward, on mission.

Because of the complaints of thirst from a traveling companion, episode fourteen [V-14] has Francis on his knees asking God to provide water. Like Moses striking the rock because of the complaints of the Israelites, the Lord God provides water which also miraculously gushes forth from a nearby rock for Francis.

Episode fifteen [V-15] shows the famous scene of

Francis preaching to the birds. Unfortunately, the upper layer of paint, called dry fresco, has faded after several hundred years. Yet, we can still tell from their shapes that these birds are not of the same species. At this point it must also be appreciated that Francis' association with animals never simply meant he was a nature lover. Francis loved the God *who created nature*. These birds actually represent all people, all personalities, nationalities and characteristics, gathered in the single diverse flock of humanity to listen to the preaching of the Gospel.

Because nothing is painted in Renaissance art in a haphazard fashion, the reason we have two nature scenes on this back wall is for a very specific reason.

When people enter a church they usually face forward until time to leave. But as they depart, the last scenes they remember are those which are closest to the doors [V-14,15]. The master designer of this artistic theology is exhorting his audience to remember that the greatest art work that we possess is actually framed in our doorway, nature itself, the divine canvas. Adding to this mission exhortation we remember that the symbolic society of the Middle Ages could have never conceived that a doorway would interrupt the encircling stories of Saint Francis. Instead of seeing two nature scenes on either side of the doors, they would have seen three nature scenes, we are just walking into one of them. We are being called not to forget to take these idealistic stories back home into our real lives. We are called not only to take care of nature, but to take care of each other. We are called to see God a little more real in each and every person than when we first walked into this church. We, like Francis, are being called to preach the Good News to all of creation. [See back cover.]

As the pilgrim leaves through the front doors of the upper basilica one may be struck by a particular design hedged in the front lawn. The *tau cross*, a common symbol of the Franciscan Order, and encountered all over Assisi, deserves explanation.

The early Christian writers commenting on the Bible would have used its Greek version called the "Septuagint" In this Greek translation of the Hebrew scriptures

(which Christians call the "Old Testament) the last letter of the Hebrew alphabet - the *tau* - was transcribed as a T.

For Christians the T came to represent the cross of Christ as being the fulfillment of the Old Testament promises. The stylized T cross, as prefigured in the last letter of the Hebrew alphabet, also represented the means by which Christ reversed the disobedience of the old Adam and became our Savior as the "New Adam."

During the Middle Ages, the religious community of Anthony the Hermit, with which Saint Francis was familiar, was very involved in the care of lepers. These men used Christ's cross shaped like the Greek T as an amulet for warding off the plague and other skin diseases. After his conversion, Francis worked with these religious in the Assisi area. He eventually accepted and adapted the T as his own crest and signature. For Francis, the T represented life-long fidelity to the passion of Christ, it was his pledge to serve the least, the leper and outcast of his day.

The *tau* imagery was intensified when Pope Innocent III opened the Fourth Lateran Council in 1215, using the exhortation of the Old Testament prophet Ezekiel (9:4), *"We are called to reform our lives, to stand in the presence of God as righteous people. God will know us by the sign of the tau marked on our foreheads."* This symbolic imagery, used by the same pope who commissioned Francis' new community a brief five years earlier, was immediately taken to heart as the friars' call to reform. With arms outstretched, Francis often told his fellow friars that their religious habit was in the shape of the *tau*, meaning that they were to become "walking crucifixes," models of a compassionate God and examples of faithfulness until their dying day.

Today, followers of Francis, as laity or religious, would wear the tau cross as an exterior sign, a "seal" of their own commitment, a remembrance of the victory of Christ over evil through daily self-sacrificing love. The sign of contradiction has become the sign of hope.